Kauai Travel Guide:

Exploring the Enchanted Shores, Secluded Sands, and Ancient Customs of Hawaii's Wild Gem with a Local's Insight

By:
Jex Meridian

in this document, including but not limited to - errors, omissions, or inaccuracies.

Table of Contents

Introduction

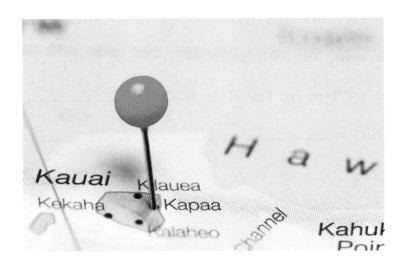

Nestled amidst the turquoise waters of the Pacific Ocean, Kauai is a tropical paradise like no other. With its lush landscapes, cascading waterfalls, pristine beaches, and vibrant culture, this enchanting Hawaiian island beckons travelers from around the world. If you've ever dreamt of embarking on a journey to an idyllic destination where adventure meets serenity, then you've just stumbled upon the most comprehensive guide to the best-kept secret in the Pacific. Welcome to "Kauai Travel guide: Your Ultimate Travel Guide to Paradise."

Prepare to be captivated, as we take you on a journey through the heart of Kauai, unveiling its hidden treasures, sharing insider tips, and revealing the unparalleled beauty that makes it a traveler's haven. From the moment you open these pages, you'll be transported to a world where emerald valleys meet cerulean skies, where ancient traditions blend seamlessly with modern luxuries, and where every sunrise paints a masterpiece on the canvas of your soul.

In this guide, we've painstakingly curated the very best of Kauai's offerings, ensuring you experience the island's magic in all its glory. Whether you're an adventurous soul seeking adrenaline-pumping escapades or a soul in search of tranquility on pristine shores, Kauai has something exceptional to offer you. From the mystical Na Pali Coast to the verdant landscapes of Waimea Canyon, from the vibrant culture of Hanalei Bay to the serenity of Polihale Beach, Kauai is a symphony of experiences waiting to be explored.

But why is this the guide you absolutely must have? Because it's not just a guide; it's your passport to an unforgettable journey. We've scoured every corner of the island, engaging with locals, discovering hidden gems, and crafting itineraries that cater to all tastes and preferences. Whether you're a first-time traveler or a seasoned explorer, this guide will ensure you make the most of your Kauai adventure.

So, get ready to immerse yourself in the magic of Kauai, where every page of "Kauai Unveiled" is a promise of unforgettable moments, and every chapter unfolds a new dimension of paradise. Let your wanderlust be your guide, and let Kauai be your destination of a lifetime. Turn the page and step into the enchantment that is "Kauai Unveiled." Your adventure awaits, and it begins here.

Chapter 1:
Travel Essentials

Best time to visit.

Known as Hawaii's "Garden Isle," Kauai is best visited at a time that suits your interests and the kind of experience you're hoping to have. Although the weather in Kauai is generally temperate and pleasant throughout the year, there are a few things to keep in mind:

1. **Weather:** All year long, Kauai experiences warm, tropical weather. But the island has two distinct seasons:
   - **Dry Season (April to October):** Weather is usually more consistent and sunnier during this time. These months are perfect for outdoor pursuits like hiking, snorkeling, and seeing the island's natural beauty because the trade winds are frequently calmer during these times.
   - **Wet Season (November to March):** The rainier season on Kauai can occasionally bring heavy rains and more humidity. While the island is still lush and lovely at this time of year, it's crucial to be ready for the likelihood of rain if you travel there during the winter.
2. **Crowds:** In the off-peak seasons of late spring (April to June) and early fall, Kauai is typically less congested (September to October). These times are fantastic options if you want a quieter, more peaceful trip.
3. **Whale Watching:** The best time to go is in the winter, namely from December to April, if you want to go whale watching. During this time, humpback whales travel to

the warm waters near Hawaii, and you may frequently see them off the coast of Kauai.

4. **Surfing:** When visiting Kauai, surfers may choose to go in the winter when the north shores experience bigger swells. Be careful, too, that this may also result in heavier surf and possibly hazardous conditions for beginners.

5. **Budget:** Consider your budget, as prices for accommodations and flights may vary throughout the year. High season (late December to early April) tends to be more expensive, so if you're looking for cost-effective options, consider the shoulder seasons.

What to pack.

Packing for a trip to Kauai, Hawaii requires careful consideration of the island's tropical climate, outdoor activities, and the overall relaxed atmosphere. Here's a comprehensive packing list to ensure you're prepared for your Kauai adventure:

1. **Lightweight Clothing:**
   - T-shirts, tank tops, and lightweight, breathable shirts
   - Shorts, skirts, and comfortable casual pants
   - Sundresses or resort wear for dining out
   - Swimsuits and cover-ups
2. **Footwear:**
   - Comfortable sandals or flip-flops for beach and casual wear
   - Sturdy, comfortable walking shoes for hiking and exploring
   - Water shoes for activities like snorkeling and kayaking
3. **Outerwear:**

- Light rain jacket or poncho for occasional rain showers, especially if visiting in the wet season (November to March)
- A light sweater or long-sleeve shirt for cooler evenings

4. **Beach Gear:**
   - Beach towels
   - Beach bag or tote
   - Sun hat and sunglasses
   - Sunscreen (reef-safe if possible)
   - Beach toys (if traveling with children)

5. **Outdoor Adventure Gear:**
   - Daypack or backpack for hiking and excursions
   - Water-resistant backpack cover or dry bags for protecting your belongings
   - Lightweight, moisture-wicking clothing for hiking
   - Hat with a brim for sun protection
   - Insect repellent

6. **Snorkeling and Water Activities:**
   - Snorkel gear (you can rent it on the island, but if you have your own, it may be more comfortable)
   - Rashguard or wetsuit for extended water activities
   - Waterproof phone pouch or camera for underwater photos

7. **Electronics:**
   - Smartphone and charger
   - Camera or waterproof action camera
   - Power bank for recharging devices on the go

8. **Personal Items:**
   - Toiletries (shampoo, conditioner, soap, etc.) - Remember that some accommodations may provide these.
   - Prescription medications
   - Personal hygiene items

- Travel-sized first-aid kit
9. **Documents and Essentials:**
   - Passport or ID
   - Travel insurance information
   - Flight tickets and travel itinerary
   - Accommodation reservations
   - Credit/debit cards and cash (Kauai has ATMs and accepts major credit cards, but it's good to have some cash on hand for smaller purchases)
   - Travel adapter and converter for charging devices
10. **Miscellaneous:**
    - Reusable water bottle (to stay hydrated)
    - Travel guidebook or maps of Kauai
    - Books or e-reader for downtime
    - Travel pillow for long flights or car rides

Getting there and moving around.

Getting to Kauai and moving around the island is relatively straightforward, but it's essential to plan your transportation options in advance to make the most of your trip. Here's a guide to help you navigate your way to and around Kauai:

Getting to Kauai:

1. **By Air:** Most travelers to Kauai arrive by air at Lihue Airport (LIH). Lihue Airport is the primary airport on the island and is served by various domestic airlines. You can book a direct flight to Lihue from several major U.S. cities, including Los Angeles, San Francisco, Seattle, and Honolulu (if you're already in Hawaii). Once you arrive at Lihue Airport, you can rent a car or arrange transportation to your accommodation.

2. **Inter-Island Flights:** If you're already in Hawaii and plan to visit Kauai from another Hawaiian island, you can book inter-island flights to Lihue or use smaller commuter airlines. These flights are relatively short and frequent.

Moving Around Kauai:

1. **Rental Cars:** Renting a car is the most convenient way to explore Kauai, as it provides you with the flexibility to visit different parts of the island at your own pace. Several car rental agencies are available at Lihue Airport and in major towns like Kapaa and Hanalei. Be sure to book your rental car in advance, especially during peak tourist seasons.
2. **Shuttle Services:** Some hotels and resorts offer shuttle services to and from the airport. If you're staying at one of these properties, check if they provide airport transfers.
3. **Taxis and Rideshares:** Taxis are available on Kauai, primarily around the airport and in larger towns. You can also use rideshare services like Uber and Lyft, but availability may be limited compared to major cities.
4. **Public Transportation:** Kauai does have a limited public bus system called "The Kauai Bus," which serves many parts of the island. While it's an economical option, the schedule may not be as frequent or convenient as a rental car.
5. **Biking:** Kauai offers scenic biking routes, and some rental shops provide bicycles for exploring coastal paths and towns. However, keep in mind that Kauai's terrain can be hilly in some areas.

6. **Walking:** In some towns, such as Kapaa and Hanalei, you can easily explore on foot. Many attractions, restaurants, and shops are within walking distance in these areas.
7. **Tours and Excursions:** Consider booking guided tours or excursions for specific activities, such as snorkeling, hiking, or boat trips. Tour operators often provide transportation to and from your accommodation.

Practical Information for Visitors

Language and communication

Visiting Kauai, Hawaii, is a fantastic experience, and communication is generally straightforward for English-speaking visitors. Here are some key points about language and communication for visitors in Kauai:

1. English is the Official Language: English is the official language of Hawaii, including Kauai. You'll find that the majority of the population speaks English fluently.

2. Hawaiian Phrases: While English is the primary language, you may come across some Hawaiian phrases and words. Learning a few basic Hawaiian words and phrases can enhance your experience and show respect for the local culture. Here are a few useful ones:

- "Aloha" – This versatile word means hello, goodbye, love, and more.
- "Mahalo" – Thank you.
- "Ohana" – Family.
- "Hale" – House or home.

3. Multicultural Population: Kauai, like the rest of Hawaii, has a diverse population, including people of Native Hawaiian, Japanese, Filipino, and other ethnic backgrounds. You may hear different languages spoken due to this diversity, but English is still the primary means of communication.

4. Tourist-Friendly Services: Kauai is a popular tourist destination, so you'll find that most people who work in the tourism industry, including hotels, restaurants, and tour operators, speak fluent English. They are accustomed to assisting visitors from around the world.

5. Communication Tips:

- Politeness and respect are highly valued in Hawaiian culture. Using phrases like "Aloha" and "Mahalo" can go a long way in building positive interactions with locals.
- Be patient and relaxed in your communication style. The pace of life in Kauai is generally slower, and people appreciate a laid-back and friendly attitude.

6. Communication Technology: Kauai has modern communication infrastructure, including mobile phone networks and internet access. You should have no trouble staying connected while on the island.

7. Emergency Services: In case of emergencies, dial 911 for police, fire, or medical assistance. The emergency services personnel typically speak English.

8. Navigating with GPS: If you're renting a car and plan to explore the island independently, having a GPS or a mobile navigation app can be extremely helpful.

9. Maps and Signage: Road signs and public signage in Kauai are typically in English, making it easy to navigate around the island.

Currency and banking

Currency and banking in Kauai, like the rest of Hawaii and the United States, are straightforward for visitors. Here's what you need to know:

Currency: The currency used in Kauai is the United States Dollar (USD), just like in the mainland United States. You can use U.S. dollars for all transactions on the island, and credit cards are widely accepted at hotels, restaurants, shops, and tourist attractions.

Banking Services: Kauai has a well-developed banking system, and you'll find various banks, credit unions, and ATMs across the island. Here are some essential banking and financial services details for visitors:

1. **ATMs:** Automated Teller Machines (ATMs) are widely available in Kauai, especially in major towns and tourist areas. You can use your debit or credit card to withdraw cash in U.S. dollars. Be aware that some ATMs may charge fees for withdrawals if they are not operated by your bank, so check with your bank regarding any potential fees.
2. **Banks:** Major national banks like Bank of Hawaii, First Hawaiian Bank, and American Savings Bank have

branches on Kauai. These banks offer a range of services, including currency exchange, although currency exchange services are less common in Hawaii than in some other tourist destinations.

3. **Credit Cards:** Credit cards, including Visa, MasterCard, American Express, and Discover, are widely accepted throughout Kauai. It's a convenient and secure way to make payments. Just be sure to notify your bank or credit card company of your travel plans to avoid any potential card issues.

4. **Traveler's Checks:** Traveler's checks are becoming less common and may not be accepted as widely as they once were. It's advisable to carry U.S. currency or use credit/debit cards for most transactions.

5. **Currency Exchange:** While some banks on Kauai may offer currency exchange services, it's generally more convenient to arrive with U.S. dollars. You can exchange your currency for U.S. dollars at airports, major international airports on the mainland U.S., or at currency exchange offices before your trip.

6. **Tipping:** Tipping is customary in Hawaii. In restaurants, it's customary to leave a tip of around 15-20% of the bill's total. Hotel staff, tour guides, and taxi drivers also appreciate tips for their services.

7. **Currency Conversion Apps:** If you're concerned about currency conversion, consider using currency conversion apps or websites to help you understand the value of the U.S. dollar in your home currency. This can be useful for budgeting and understanding prices while you're on the island.

Overall, visitors to Kauai will find that banking and currency transactions are convenient and straightforward, making it easy to manage your finances during your stay on the island.

Safety

Kauai is generally considered a safe destination for visitors, but like any place, it's essential to be aware of safety precautions and potential risks. Here are some safety tips for visitors to Kauai:

1. **Water Safety:**
    *   While the beaches of Kauai are beautiful, they can have strong currents and waves. Always pay attention to posted warning signs and follow lifeguard instructions.
    *   If you're not an experienced swimmer, avoid entering the ocean in areas with rough surf.
    *   When snorkeling or engaging in water activities, be cautious of coral reefs and marine life. Do not touch or disturb coral, as it is fragile and can cause injury.
2. **Hiking and Outdoor Activities:**
    *   Kauai offers stunning hiking trails, but some can be challenging and potentially dangerous, especially during adverse weather conditions. Always check the weather forecast before setting out on a hike.
    *   Inform someone of your hiking plans, including your expected return time and the trail you intend to explore.

- Carry enough water, wear appropriate clothing and footwear, and bring essential supplies when hiking.

3. **Wildlife:**
   - Kauai is home to a variety of wildlife, including birds and seals. Maintain a safe distance and do not disturb or feed them.
   - Be cautious when swimming in areas where sharks are known to frequent, and follow any posted warnings.

4. **Sun Protection:**
   - The Hawaiian sun can be intense. Wear sunscreen with a high SPF, sunglasses, and a wide-brimmed hat to protect yourself from sunburn.
   - Stay hydrated by drinking plenty of water, especially if you're engaging in outdoor activities.

5. **Respect Local Customs and Culture:**
   - Be respectful of the local Hawaiian culture and traditions. Ask for permission before entering private property, and do not remove rocks or shells from sacred sites.
   - Observe and appreciate the local customs and practices, such as the hula and lei-making.

6. **Crime and Personal Safety:**
   - Kauai is generally a safe place, but like anywhere, exercise common sense. Lock your car, hotel room, and keep valuables secure.
   - Avoid leaving belongings unattended on beaches or in public areas.

7. **COVID-19 Precautions (if applicable):**

- Keep up-to-date with any COVID-19 restrictions or guidelines in place during your visit. This may include mask-wearing, social distancing, and vaccination requirements.

8. **Emergency Services:**
   - Familiarize yourself with emergency phone numbers, including 911 for immediate assistance.

Chapter 2:
Must Visit Places in Kauai

Kauai is divided into four shores.

- South shore
- West shore
- East shore
- North shore

Here are the top twenty things to do before traveling to each shore:

- The gorgeous Na Pali Coast, known for its lofty cliffs, lush valleys, and breathtaking views, can be explored by boat or on foot.
- Discover Waimea Canyon, the "Grand Canyon of the Pacific," with its vibrant red and green cliffs, waterfalls, and panoramic views.
- Relax on the beautiful crescent-shaped beach in Hanalei Bay, which is bordered by lush mountains and dotted with tiny beach towns.
- On a challenging but rewarding trek, discover the Kalalau Trail, which provides stunning views of the Na Pali Coast and undiscovered beaches.

- Wailua River: Kayak or go on a boat tour along the picturesque Wailua River to see places like Fern Grotto and Secret Falls.
- Poipu Beach: Take advantage of the sunny shoreline at Poipu Beach, where you may swim, snorkel, surf, or simply relax.
- View the breathtaking vistas of the North Shore while exploring the opulent and historically significant Limahuli Garden, which is home to native Hawaiian plants.
- Discover how coffee beans are grown and roasted by visiting Kauai Coffee Company and taking a tour of the largest coffee farm on the island.
- Watch the Spouting Horn natural phenomenon, where powerful waves cause a lava tube to erupt in a magnificent spray.
- Visit the charming village of Hanapepe, known for its historic buildings, art galleries, and Friday Night Art Walk.
- Kilauea Lighthouse: Take
- Tunnels Beach: Scuba or snorkel at Tunnels Beach, which is well-known for its colorful coral reefs, tropical fish, and sporadic sightings of sea turtles.
- Visit Koke'e State Park to explore the varied ecosystems, stroll along the trails, stop at viewpoint sites, and learn about unusual plant and animal species.
- Smith's Tropical Paradise: Enjoy a classic Hawaiian luau with authentic food, live music, hula dancing, and fire performances at Smith's Tropical Paradise.
- Hanalei Valley Lookout: Visit this viewpoint to take in the view of the Hanalei Valley, taro fields, and flowing Hanalei River.

- Polihale State Park: Travel to Kauai's westernmost point and unwind on Polihale State Park's wide beach, which is renowned for its beautiful sunsets and golden beaches.
- Maha'ulepu Heritage Trail: Travel along the Maha'ulepu Heritage Trail for a beautiful coastal stroll as you pass craggy cliffs, sand dunes, and historic Hawaiian monuments.
- The Kauai Museum, which offers exhibitions, artifacts, and educational activities, is a great place to learn about the island's past, present, and future.
- An exciting helicopter trip will give you a bird's-eye perspective of Kauai's breathtaking landscapes, including waterfalls, canyons, and secluded valleys.

Lets explore each shore;

West Shore

Waimea Hawaiian Church

Want to hear some heartfelt spiritual hymns being sung? Not everyone will like this. visit Hawaii's church. On Sunday, it begins at nine. There won't likely be any other mainlanders present. Everything is in Hawaiian, so you won't understand a word. When they sing harmoniously while standing stationary, you get chicken skin (Hawaiian slang for goose bumps). As a gesture of aloha, place some money in the collection container. On the ocean side of the main road in Waimea, there is a white building that serves as the local church.

Most navigation systems are, for whatever reason, in stealth mode; if you discover Wrangler's Steakhouse or Big Save in Waimea, you're there.

Hanapepe Art Night

In the little village of Hanapepe, "art night" is held every Friday from 5 to 9 p.m. In addition to the fact that all the shops stay open late, there are food trucks, street vendors, and music (well, 9 p.m. is late by Kauai standards). Many of the local artists are present in the stores to engage with consumers and sell their works. There is a wonderful bookstore there as well (see Talk Story Bookstore). Enjoy Art Night and think about purchasing some jewelry or a tiny etching, but remember that it's incredibly subtle and not for everyone.

Locate the footbridge that crosses the river (it is next to Talk Story Bookstore and is located between two structures). Standing there and looking at

Talk Story Bookstore

If you like to read or even if you don't, stop by Talk Story in Hanapepe. In theory, Kekaha won't receive one; they claim to be the most western independent bookseller in the nation. You can go to Talk Story whenever you choose, and while you're there, you can attend Hanapepe Art Night.

Ed Justus, the store's proprietor, would likely greet you when you entered and offer to give you a tour. Yes, please! You're likely to discover something new there because of their eclectic and carefully picked selection. They also present humorous gifts.

Helpful hint: The expression "talk story" is Hawaiian slang for "shoot the breeze" or idle chitchat. It does not imply spreading rumors or disparaging others because that is "talk stink." Being such a small island, Kauai is hardly the place to talk trash. That is a generally sound rule.

Tasting Kauai

This is a sampling tour that stops at various eateries and retail establishments, providing tasting samples and information at each stop. Numerous spots all throughout Kauai are where Tasting Kauai offers excursions. The only walking tour in Hanapepe is the West Shore tour; all other tours need you to get in your car and drive to the next destination.

You will enjoy the strolling because it will provide you with some exercise in between courses and give you more opportunity to converse with your tour guide and other tourists. The enormous serving sizes at each stop will surprise you; they build up to a full lunch spread out over a few hours. In addition to talking to the restaurant and business owners, guides can provide information on the history of Hanapepe town.

Tasting Kauai provides a portion of its earnings to regional food banks on the island of Kauai. The cuisine is of the highest quality and is sourced locally whenever feasible.

On Friday, the West Shore tour concludes shortly before Hanapepe Art Night kicks out, allowing you to preserve your fantastic parking location and stick around for Talk Story Books and Art Night.

Kauai Kookie Factory Store

Even though Kauai Kookies are sold in shops all over the island, if you go to the production plant in Hanapepe, you can find a huge selection of flavors and patterns that aren't frequently offered. They provide away free samples. It is worthwhile to stop in if you like sweets and are already in Hanapepe.

Only the retail store is accessible for tours, despite the fact that it is the real factory where they are made.

Salty Wahine

This small store is located in Hanapepe near to the Kauai Kookie Factory Store. Woman is pronounced "wah HEEN ay." They have a variety of salts and sugars with unique flavors that are manufactured in-house in the back of the store. You'll adore their hot lava on almost anything and their guava garlic salt on meat. Don't worry if you run out at home because you can get more from their website.

Refillable grinders are a smart idea, as you know. The grinding improves the spice's adhesion to food and increases its penetration.

Waimea Canyon

On the Hawaiian island of Kauai, there is a beautiful natural wonder called Waimea Canyon. It is frequently referred to as the "Grand Canyon of the Pacific" and is a well-liked vacation spot for those who enjoy the outdoors and the natural world.

The following are some significant Waimea Canyon facts:

Location: Waimea Canyon is located in Waimea Canyon State Park on the western side of Kauai. Waimea's town makes it simple to get there by automobile.

Geology and Formation: The Waimea River and the fall of the volcano that originally gave rise to Kauai eroded the canyon over the course of millions of years, forming it. The varied mineral deposits in the rocks are what give the canyon walls their vivid hues, which range from red to green.

Waimea Canyon is one mile (1.6 kilometers) wide, measures around 14 miles (22.5 kilometers) in length, and has a depth of 3,600 feet (1,100 meters). It is a magnificent sight due to its size and contrasting hues. The canyon's natural beauty is enhanced by its luxuriant foliage, waterfalls, and variety of flora and wildlife.

Trails and hiking: Waimea Canyon has a variety of trails for hikers of all levels of experience. The Canyon Trail, Cliff Trail, and Awaawapuhi Trail are a few of the well-known trails. These routes offer chances to discover the canyon's distinctive topography and take in expansive views of the surroundings.

Lookouts: Along State Highway 550, the main thoroughfare, there are several viewing sites that provide breathtaking views of the canyon. The Waimea Canyon Lookout, which offers a sweeping view of the canyon's vastness and the nearby Na Pali Coast, is the most well-known vantage point.

Weather: Because the weather in Waimea Canyon is unpredictable, it is best to be prepared. The canyon's higher elevations may be colder and wetter than its coastal regions. When organizing your visit, it's a good idea to look up the weather forecast and pack appropriately.

At some point during your journey, you have to make sure to drive up the Waimea Canyon and check out the views. If you can arrive at the final viewpoint (Pu'u o Kila) early in the day, your chances of seeing anything amazing will be higher. You can find yourself simply staring into a cloud bank later on in the day and wondering what the fuss is about.

Visitor advice: If you're going to Waimea Canyon, you should pack water, sunscreen, and insect repellent. It's also a good idea to wear sneakers or hiking boots that are comfortable. To protect the fragile ecosystem, keep to the pathways that have been established and respect the environment.

Overall, a trip to Waimea Canyon is a special experience that gives you the chance to take in Kauai's natural beauty and take in its breathtaking magnificence.

South Shore

Makauwahi Cave

It is known for its cultural and scientific significance as one of Hawaii's largest limestone caverns because it has provided crucial information about the island's natural history and human habitation.

Among other geological processes, freshwater and saltwater eroded the local limestone to form the cave. The "Great Room," a huge room with numerous chambers and tunnels, is where the main entrance opens.

Archaeological digs in Makauwahi Cave have produced a plethora of artifacts and fossils that show past human activities and the ecological history of the island. Layers of silt that have collected over thousands of years are preserved in the cave, providing a unique record of environmental change.

Ancient stone tools, pottery shards, and plant remains have all been found at Makauwahi Cave and show that Native Hawaiian communities once existed there hundreds of years ago. The Kauai mole duck and the Kauai 'o'o are two extinct bird species whose fossils have been found in the cave.

With continued attempts to explore its geological and archaeological significance, Makauwahi Cave has emerged as a significant location for research and teaching. The cave is a component of the Makauwahi Cave Reserve, which also includes a limestone sinkhole and a system of coastal dunes, as well as a surrounding area with numerous different habitats.

Visitors can take guided tours of the reserve to explore the cave and learn about its significance for science and culture. It offers a rare chance to observe how closely people and the environment have interacted throughout Kauai's history.

To reach this fascinating spot, which is an active archeological site, follow the beach directions for Maha'ulepu Beaches. You must crouch down and enter a little rock tunnel even though the collapsed cave is open to the air. There won't be a chain barring the entrance in the field to your right if the cave is open to the public (just past the light blue shack). Daily 10–2 guided tours are available (or until 4 on Sunday). But keep in mind that this is Kauai, so don't make any firm plans. Maha'ulepu may be closed, yet it is still accessible.

Spouting Horn

This blowhole is a natural waterspout that is brought about by wave motion.

The Spouting Horn is located in the Poipu neighborhood of Kauai, next to Lawai Road and a short distance to the east of Poipu Beach Park. It has a designated parking lot and is easily reached by automobile.

Geological Formation: When ocean waves strike an undersea lava tube or tunnel, the spouting effect is produced. Water shoots up through a small opening as it rushes into the tube and pressure builds, creating a stunning spray of water and mist.

The attraction is situated in Spouting Horn Park, which has a gorgeous seaside scenery, restrooms, a grassy picnic area, and a few merchants selling trinkets and regional crafts. Visitors can take in the beautiful surroundings, observe the spouting activity, and explore the local tide pools.

Chanting and Legend: The Spouting Horn, according to Hawaiian tradition, is thought to be a mo'o, or a large lizard, that a local fisherman once captured inside the lava tube. The spout's loud hissing noise is thought to be the mo'o's roar. Locals frequently chant and blow conch shells, which adds to the site's ethereal atmosphere.

Safety Advice: Although the Spouting Horn is a magnificent sight, it is important to take precautions when going. The blowhole spray can be powerful, so it's best to maintain a safe distance and take a step back. To prevent any mishaps, stay away from the edge and stay off the rocks.

Visitors to the island should not miss the Kauai Spouting Horn, which offers a rare natural spectacle and a window into Hawaiian mythology. Respect the area, abide by any posted signs or instructions, and take in the breathtaking coastline scenery.

About a mile away, across from the Poipu roundabout, is the entrance to Allerton and McBryde Gardens. If you're already in the area, have a look. In addition, the region is home to several chicken families (birds, not people), as well as shops that sell commodities.

You can get a wonderful view of the water by continuing past Spouting Horn to the end of the road and turning around at the gate. Stop your car to the side and watch the spectacle. Native plants have been encouraged and restored in this area. In the spring, whales give birth to their calves close to this coast.

Turtles in Whaler's Cove

There is a considerable probability you will see turtles in the waters at Whaler's Cove when it comes to turtles. The coastal seas of Kauai are frequently home to the Hawaiian green sea turtle, or honu. Because of their placid disposition, people frequently encounter these turtles swimming close to the coast or sunbathing on sandy beaches.

It's crucial to keep in mind that sea turtles are protected by the Endangered Species Act and that it is forbidden to touch or otherwise harm them. In Whaler's Cove, if you come across a turtle while snorkeling or diving, it is recommended to keep your distance and respect its natural behavior.

At the extreme left end of their parking lot, there are stairs that down to the cove. Disregard the trespassing signs. The cove is open to everyone; those signs are only for the uninitiated. Leave your automobile in the street if you're worried. In the fall and winter, sea turtles approach this little cove after dusk to rest. There are a lot of them (in the fall, and in November and December too). The hour or so before dusk is the best time to visit. If the surf and wind are particularly calm when they come up for air, you can hear them inhale. Magical.

If you intend to travel to Whaler's Cove or any other area where sea turtles are found, be sure to engage in responsible tourism and abide by local ordinances to safeguard these lovely animals and their habitat.

Kauai Coffee

You can explore the coffee farm on your own, find out how coffee is cultivated and processed, and sample some of their coffees.

The Kauai Coffee Estate, which offers tours of the plantation, is another place visitors to Kauai can go. From planting and harvesting through roasting and packaging, the trips give participants an understanding of the coffee-growing process. Both visitors and coffee connoisseurs enjoy visiting it.

Due to its dedication to environmentally friendly agricultural methods, Kauai Coffee has achieved notoriety. To lessen their influence on the environment, they use strategies including water conservation, recycling, and the use of renewable energy sources.

In general, Kauai Coffee is renowned for producing fine, flavorful coffee that highlights the distinctive features of the Kauai region.

They also have one of the best gift shops, which has both common and uncommon products.

Allerton and McBryde Gardens

Whether you like plants or not, this website is great. At the end of Lawai Road from the Poipu roundabout, it is a section of the National Tropical Botanical Garden and is situated right across from Spouting Horn.

Plants, flowers, trees, fruit, statues, and other things are there. All of the tour guides are very knowledgable and hospitable, but Sam is particularly exceptional.

Try their self-guided "Behind the Scenes" tour, which includes a trip to the plant nursery and a stroll to a pond in the top garden. However, there are frequently guides roaming the area who will give you an impromptu lecture. They are developing a part with traditional canoe plants and structures in this lovely location.

Before boarding the bus, stock up on bug juice in the waiting room.

Our suggestion for a great evening is the Allerton Sunset Tour. Make a reservation because it might not be available every day. You get to explore parts of the garden that aren't included in the standard tours, like the seashore and home of Allerton. Dinner is included in the excursion. Robert Allerton was a wealthy guy who loved art and nature, and he created and built the entire estate. His tale is really intriguing. The laws would not let him to leave his estate to the guy he loved and shared a home with. Robert thus took him in as his "son". That gap was immediately plugged by the authorities.

Advice: The Allerton trips are somewhat expensive. If it helps, your money helps them with their preservation and education efforts, and it might even be tax deductible (ask your bean counter). They frequently give discount codes if you book online at least one day in advance.

Ziplining with Outfitters Kauai

This zipline trip is enjoyable. Try the Adrenaline Tour, which features a high-speed zipline across the valley that you can ride prone like "Superman" and concludes with a short T-bar line into a swimming hole. The guides are extremely thorough and cautious while also using an odd mixture of smart-ass safety-related comedy. Instead of their Poipu round-about location, Outfitter Kauai's tour departs from their Kipu Ranch facility on Kipu Road.

Recommendation: Check out ziplining at Princeville Ranch if you're up on the north coast.

Hyatt Hotel

You'll like making your way down to the beach through the lobby, which features exotic birds, a decent coffee shop, and lots of comfortable chairs. There are numerous lagunas for swimming, pathways, and seats to discover. Go picnicking! If you're cool about it and hide your non-Hyatt towels while swimming, the employees might assume you're staying there. If it helps, you can help them out by purchasing a $15 mai tai at the bar.

Tip: You can also park at Shipwreck Beach (see Beaches) and enter the Hyatt lagoon area by walking through the gate.

There is a waterslide, but in order to use it, you must have a hotel wristband.

Advice: Accents is a convenience store located immediately outside the lobby. The costs are oddly reasonable and it's nice and cool.

Kauai Humane Society – Dog Field Trip

Just west of Lihue on Highway 50 is a contemporary structure home to the Kauai Humane Society. They'll let you borrow one for a field trip in order to aid the socialization and adoption of their canines. You'll receive a towel, leash, snacks, and a cool "Adopt Me" vest (for the dog, not you). You can go on an expedition with the dog for an hour or all day. When meeting residents and other guests, mentioning that you have a dog is a terrific conversation starter.

Advice: Every day but Wednesday is acceptable for a field excursion.

East Shore

Luau at Smith's Tropical Paradise

Try a luau at Smith's Tropical Paradise in Wailua. It is situated in a nice garden region, and you can ride a tram there for a tour of the local wildlife and flowers while being given narration (including peacocks). The cuisine is typical all-you-can-eat luau stuff, and the mai tais are poor but plentiful. They'll allow you to fully appreciate the cheesy but frequently beautiful dancing show that comes after dinner. Make a reservation.

Advice: Long tables are used for family-style sitting. For groups of six or more, they will reserve spots; smaller groups must find their own seats.

To avoid eating poi alone, follow this advice. Into it, dip some kalua pork. Ono!

Grove Farm Museum Tour

This location is hidden away in Lihue, next to Safeway and Costco. You'd never guess that the area contains 100 acres of grounds and historic dwellings, including the original homes of the Wilcox family. A fascinating peek at the past and way of life of an early sugar plantation family may be found on the guided walking tour. In addition, they have a huge collection of documents, books, and artifacts that date back to the late 1970s, when the last member of the Wilcox family lived there.

Kauai Hindu Monastery

A Hindu temple is being built by hand by craftsmen out of granite, however this is only briefly mentioned in UKG. Even after decades of work, they are still not finished. You can visit the lovely gardens at any time, but you must make a reservation by contacting 888-735-1619 in order to take the free tour and see the stone temple itself (because parking is so scarce). You will gain some knowledge about Hinduism and their endeavor. You must wear modestly; shawls are available for loan if necessary.

Douse yourself in bug repellant before entering. For whatever reason, those Hindu mosquitoes are very aggressive.

Coconut Coasters - Bike Rentals

The Coconut Coasters store is located on the ocean side at the northernmost part of Kapa'a. The trail has only slight inclines, the bikes are incredibly smooth and easy to peddle, and the coastal vistas are stunning when you ride in the direction of the north. Even a basket is available for carrying your belongings. The minimal amount of time is an hour, but if you want to explore both directions and make stops, allow two hours. Since there isn't much cover along the trail and the hot sun can burn you, you might want to pick the morning or afternoon.

You can earn a discount if you're sporting Seattle Seahawks apparel or if you successfully exclaim "Go Hawks!" to the merchant.

Kayaking on Wailua River

To get to the trailhead, you kayak up the (extremely calm) Wailua River. After that, you hike in to Secret Falls for lunch. a lot of fun.

They warn you not to stand beneath the falls because rocks could fall and hit you in the head. It's a lot of fun.

Koloa Rum Tasting

Need some free alcohol? (Well, a gram.) Visit the Koloa Rum Company at the Lihue-area Kilohana Plantation. They offer a great gift shop with loads of rum-related items, and you should check out their free rum tastings; just sign up at the counter. One of the remaining relics of the sugarcane plantation economy, their rum is produced from sugarcane cultivated on the island of Kauai. While visiting the plantation, you can stroll around the grounds, explore the iconic Gaylord's restaurant and bar, ride the extortionate train, or get some chocolate from the candy store.

Kauai Museum

The museum presents the past, present, and culture of Kauai and its inhabitants. Here are some details regarding the Kauai Museum:

Location: The Kauai Museum is located in the county seat of Kauai County, the town of Lihue. 4428 Rice Street, Lihue, Hawaii, 96766, is the address.

The museum's displays include a wide range of topics that reflect many facets of Kauai's history and culture. These include exhibits on prehistoric Hawaiian antiquities, traditional crafts, Captain James Cook's arrival, items from the plantation era, and the significance of sugar in Kauai's past. The displays provide information about the island's geological formation, early settlement, and indigenous people's traditions and customs.

Items: The Kauai Museum is home to a sizable collection of historical artifacts from Kauai. These include vintage household goods, weapons, and equipment utilized by the Native Hawaiians. The museum also features old pictures, pieces of art, and records that add more background information on the island's past.

Activities & Programs: To engage visitors and foster an awareness of Kauai's culture, the museum sponsors a number of events and programs. There may be storytelling sessions, cultural demonstrations, educational workshops, and performances of traditional music and dance among them.

Gift Store: The Kauai Museum features a gift shop where customers can buy a variety of goods, including books on Hawaiian history and culture, locally produced art, jewelry, and other Kauai-related souvenirs.

The museum is typically open Monday through Saturday from 9:00 am to 4:00 pm (hours are subject to change, so it's best to check the official website or call the museum for the most up-to-date information). There can be admission costs, and seniors, kids, and students might be eligible for discounts. The museum's website or direct contact is advised for the most recent details on opening times, admission costs, and any upcoming special events.

It is much better because your entrance fee includes a week-long pass and there are free docent presentations available a couple days a week at 10:30am.

Tubing in Irrigation Tunnels

You may go tubing through historic irrigation canals and tunnels in the interior of Kauai with Kauai Backcountry Adventures in Lihue. Although the UKG doesn't find it particularly enjoyable, you will. The active and entertaining young guides will share information about Kauai with you while you journey in the van and when you are out on the trail and canals. Through the tunnels, the water may move rather quickly, making for an exciting ride as you spin and bounce off the walls. Although the price is a little high, we would go on this unique excursion again with friends despite the price.

The guides advised against using insect repellent because the water is rushing so quickly. When the van stops at the valley lookout or before making your way down the trail to the launch point, you should rub some bug juice on your skin, particularly your ankles.

North Shore

Kilauea Lighthouse

From the road, you can see the birds soaring in the air and the peninsula of the lighthouse and the lake below. However, we advise paying the ten dollars and completing the little journey to the lighthouse if you want the full experience. There is a ton of information on the lighthouse's past available, including a video of a tour guide showcasing the structure's different elements and rotating light mechanism. You may only view the ancient structure from the exterior; guided tours are only available on Wednesdays and Saturdays. A paper map titled Kaua'i Island Atlas and Maps by Robert Seimer can be found in the small shop there along with other beautiful books and souvenirs. Awe-inspiring sights may be found all along the way.

Ziplining at Princeville Ranch

Explore Princeville Ranch Adventures right now. There are a few options open to them; they should pick the one that includes lunch at a swimming hole. They set up the tent for Kauai Ono in their front yard.

Other excursions and outdoor activities are available at Princeville Ranch, allowing guests to discover and take in Kauai's natural splendor. The ranch also provides other well-liked activities, some of which are:

1. Riding a horse: Visitors can take guided horseback riding tours to explore the ranch's gorgeous paths and take in the tranquil environment of the surrounding area.
2. Hiking & Nature Walks: Princeville Ranch offers a number of hiking and nature paths that lead tourists through stunning natural settings, such as valleys, streams, and tropical forests. These escorted hikes offer the chance to discover the island's history, flora, and fauna.
3. Kayaking & Stand-Up Paddleboarding: The ranch provides guided kayaking and stand-up paddleboarding tours on the Hanalei River so that

guests can explore the waterways and take in the peace and quiet of the area.

4. Princeville Ranch offers guided trips to the exclusive waterfalls on their property. Visitors can enjoy the spectacular cascades surrounded by lush foliage while taking a relaxing plunge in the natural pools.

The ranch emphasizes environmentally friendly procedures and encourages environmental preservation. It provides a variety of activities ideal for families, couples, and outdoor lovers seeking to commune with nature and discover Kauai's natural beauty.

Sunset Golf Cart Tour at Makai Golf Club

In essence, you arrive a few hours before dusk. The tracking system is Kauai-casual, so you need contact beforehand (808.826.1912) to get your name on the list. They appeared surprised to see us both times. While you wait to go, enjoy a shockingly inexpensive happy hour at the cantina. A golf professional will accompany you on the course while sharing tales, pointing out plants, animals, and breathtaking scenery.

Take bug juice since mosquitoes might become active as the sun sets.

Advice: You have a good chance of seeing nesting albatross parents or chicks up close if you go in the winter or spring.

Na 'Aina Kai Botanical Gardens

It is a private garden with a spectacular display of tropical plants, flowers, and landscapes spread across more than 240 acres of land.

The garden was built by Joyce and Ed Doty with the intention of preserving and sharing Kauai's natural beauty. A formal garden, a children's garden, a hardwood plantation, a moss and fern garden, a meadow, and a desert garden are just a few of the themed gardens that can be found at Na ina Kai, which translates to "Lands by the Sea" in Hawaiian.

Visitors at Naina Kai have the option of taking guided or unguided walks through the grounds. While the self-guided walks let tourists explore at their own pace, the guided tours give detailed information on the many species and sceneries. Special activities at the garden include art exhibitions, music, and educational programs.

The Sculpture Park, which houses a collection of more than 80 contemporary sculptures by renowned artists, is one of the centerpieces of Na Ina Kai Botanical Gardens. The natural surroundings of the garden are incorporated into these sculptures, resulting in a distinctive and engrossing experience.

Naina Kai also includes a lovely beachside area called "Sunset Point" in addition to the gardens. Weddings and other special events are frequently held in this region because of the breathtaking ocean vistas it affords.

But if you're staying in the north, this autonomous, nonprofit garden is extremely cool, and it's in a good spot. A guided tram tour makes stops along the way where you can get out and go for a short walk. The sculptures are amazing, and the native and invading plant species are discussed in an interesting way.

In general, Kauai's Na 'ina Kai Botanical Gardens should not be missed by nature lovers and those looking for a tranquil, enchanted setting.

Limahuli Garden

This is the third National Tropical Botanical Garden on the island of Kauai, following Allerton and McBryde Gardens on the south shore. It is located close to the end of the road on the north coast, before Ke'e Beach.

The conservation and preservation of native Hawaiian plants and ecosystems is a priority at Limahuli Garden and Preserve. It displays a wide variety of plants, including endangered and unusual species that can only be found in Hawaii. Each section of the garden represents a different Hawaiian habitat, such as a coastal, lowland, upland, or montane ecosystem.

Visitors to Limahuli Garden can stroll along the garden's trails and take in the surrounding natural splendor. The routes provide expansive views of the ocean and mountains while passing through tropical forests and over streams. Additionally, the garden offers educational activities and interpretive displays to teach visitors about local flora, customs, and the value of conservation.

This gorgeous valley is home to a wide variety of carefully maintained flora, some of which are endangered. We strongly suggest joining a guided tour. You'll learn so much more about the flora, the history of the island, the garden, and even a few Hawaiian stories for only $40 as opposed to $20. Get your drink on because there might be mosquitos in certain gloomy areas if the wind isn't blowing. Because it rains more frequently on the north coast, it's a good idea to bring an umbrella or hat. You'll easily dry off when the sun comes out again.

Advice: At 10:00 am, the escorted trips start. Depending on where you're staying, the trip requires a major time commitment because driving from Poipu will take at least 90 minutes. Do it!

Beaches

Get ready in advance for a relaxed trip that includes snorkeling. You can hire snorkeling gear by the week; just keep it in the trunk of your car to always keep it on hand. Even though you can rent gear virtually anywhere, Snorkel Bob's and Seasport Divers are dependable choices. If you are staying there, see if the resort has beach chairs (check the closet). Rent them if not, then leave them in the car! At Seasport Divers near the Poipu roundabout, there are chairs in the Tommy Bahama design that resemble backpacks. We're telling you, having chairs at the beach will make you happy.

Advice: Avoid attempting to walk while wearing fins; you risk falling and will undoubtedly be recognized as a tourist. Put your mask on first before wading out into the water while holding your fins in a sandy area until you are about waist deep. Get into the water between waves while breathing through your snorkel, then don your fins. Reverse the procedure to return to land when you're ready. When the water is shallow enough, swim until it, then kneel to take off your fins before leaving.

Keep one eye on the ocean when you're at the beach or on the rocks. You can be caught off guard by a large wave and fall. When a wave approaches when you are in the water, pivot and stand with your legs apart sideways to the wave. The likelihood of you remaining upright will be higher.

Almost every beach on Kauai might have a monk seal lazing around. At Salt Ponds, Poipu, and Beach House/Lawai Road, you can see them. It is forbidden to interfere with them in any manner since they are endangered. A rope barrier will be erected around a monk seal by a volunteer monk seal response team to warn tourists to keep their distance.

Remember that seals need a clear path to safety and advise against walking on the beach or in the shallow areas between them and the water.

There are a ton of beaches on Kauai, and UKG provides excellent descriptions. Here are a handful of the most popular ones, along with some helpful information.

South Shore

Maha'ulepu Beaches

- Lounging
- Walking
- Seclusion

Although there are several distinct beaches along this area, we just refer to it as Maha'ulepu. Let's talk about how to pronounce "mah HA leh poo." You may have a favorite beach that you frequently visit called Kawailoa Bay. It's wonderful for relaxing, reading, strolling, and shallow wading, but avoid swimming out because there isn't a reef to provide protection. There aren't any restrooms available. Here, because of their proximity to the water, the trees provide some nice shade. Kawailoa Bay doesn't see a lot of people, so you can have a stretch of the beach to yourself, especially during the workweek. There is also a fantastic trek that begins there; see Hikes and Walks.

The route to Maha'ulepu can be unsteady, but if you drive carefully and avoid the biggest potholes, your rental car should be alright. On this particular route, you'll be happy if you leased an SUV. (Once the road in Poipu turns to gravel, continue past the Hyatt. After CJM Stables, turn a couple times (the alternatives will be gated closed). You will eventually arrive at a parking space with a puddle in the center. It's Gillin's Beach here. But don't stop there; continue on the dirt road to the left until it ends at Kauailoa Bay, where there are additional parking spaces. Since the gates are locked at sunset, leave before 6 o'clock.

You will directly pass the guard shack designating the field leading to Makauwahi Cave on the rough road to Maha'ulepu.

Advice: Grove Farms, the company that owns the road that leads to Maha'ulepu, occasionally closes the road for upkeep (or for movie filming.) You can see if the road is closed as mentioned on the Makauwahi Cave website. In any case, if the road is gated, you can park at CJM Stables and enter on foot, or you can wait until a different day. The cave may be reached in approximately 10 minutes, and Kawailoa Bay in another 20. Con: entering with all of your belongings. Even greater privacy is a plus.

Beach House/Lawai Road

- Snorkeling

- Lounging
- Sunset

Just a few minutes from the Poipu roundabout, Lawai Road Beach is located alongside the road to Spouting Horn. Right in front of the Beach House restaurant is a little sandy beach. There is typically excellent snorkeling there, particularly in the winter and early in the day when the ocean is calmer. Even though "Lawai Beach" is actually a different beach in Allerton Garden, some people still refer to it as such.

Koloa Landing

- Snorkeling
- Scuba Diving

Whaler's Cove is a rocky cove with a boat ramp that is well-liked by snorkelers and divers but is not a beach. Just south of the Poipu roundabout, on Hoonani Road, is where you may locate it. The quantity of runoff from the nearby Waikomo Stream and the swell pouring in from the south determine the visibility, which is erratic. Before diving in, you can inspect it by strolling along the rocky wall that surrounds the cove and looking at the sea below. The water is rather clear if you can see the rocky bottom (polarized sunglasses are helpful here). There are several fish and sea turtles to view when the conditions are ideal.

Baby Beach

- Lounging
- Sunsets (especially winter)

This is a little neighborhood beach close to the Poipu roundabout. It's only useful for relaxing, reading, and enjoying a beverage while watching the sunset. Oh, those sound like some fun things to do! From Lawai Road, turn into Hoona Road, and follow the route between two homes to the beach. On Kauai, beaches are open to the public, and there are tucked-away access paths all around the island. Although they might not have signs, it is quite acceptable to use them. Local keiki (children) frequently play in the small lagoon during the week. In the winter, when the sun is still lowering into the lake, the sunsets here are very spectacular (in April it reaches the land). Visitors and locals alike will frequently introduce themselves to you as they congregate to have drinks while watching the entertainment. You will only ever see the green flash here.

Sheraton Beach

- Swimming
- Lounging
- Boogie boarding

The Poipu Sheraton boasts lovely gardens that are right next to the ocean. You can bring own chairs and sit along the beach, or you can find a grassy spot under the palm trees at the Sheraton or a rocking chair there. On the roadside closest to the ocean, there are public parking areas on both ends of the hotel complex.

Tip: Locate the grassy area with fire pits immediately outside RumFire. In the rockers, it's a nice place to unwind. The breeze sweeps right through, even on the warmest summer days.

Poipu Beach

- Lounging
- Sunset
- Swimming
- Snorkeling
- Lifeguard

The epitome of a Kauai beach is Poipu Beach. There are plenty of sandy beaches for relaxing and people-watching, a sheltered little lagoon for swimming, and a fantastic snorkeling spot. Yes, it is a well-known beach, but there is usually parking and a small patch of sand available. The tombolo, a stretch of sand that extends to a rocky area, is what makes Poipu Beach unique. Sometimes you may stand in the middle of the beach and have water gently lapping at your feet from both sides because the waves come in from both directions. Tombolos are extremely rare; there are reportedly just three in the entire Hawaiian archipelago, all on Kauai, and Poipu is the only one that can be reached.

The tombolo has been eroding in recent years due to storm surges, but normal wave movement ought to be putting it back together.

Brenneke's Beach

- Boogie boarding
- Lounging

Brenneke's Beach is located over to the left across the grassy area (facing the water) from Poipu Beach. Many folks come here to boogie board. It's simple to attempt boogie boarding; after checking your condo's closet, head across the street to

Nukumoi to rent the necessary equipment (a board and short flippers). Simply ensure that there are many others in the water, preferably some locals. There may be a reason why you're the only person present; the situation could be hazardous. Don't ride too far in near the shore at Brenneke's, especially where the rocks are.

Tip: Kick your fins to start moving in the same direction as the wave as it approaches you from behind. Push the front of the board down with your arms as the wave approaches you to begin sliding down the wave's "slope."

Shipwreck Beach

- Lounging
- Boogie boarding

The Hyatt Hotel is directly near to this vast, sandy beach. There, the wave movement can be very strong. Crazy people jump into the lake from a rocky point on the left.

West Side

Salt Ponds Beach Park

- Swimming
- Lounging
- Lifeguard

There is lots of space for relaxing in this attractive park, which also has a wonderful sandy beach. Although the water is safe for swimming, it is frequently too murky for decent snorkeling. There is a higher than usual likelihood of spotting a monk seal.

Polihale Beach

- Seclusion
- Sunset
- Big waves

Although some people mistakenly believe that Polihale means "home of the afterlife," it simply refers to the place where people's spirits pass on. There are not many people on the long, empty beach. We were once given the advice to "move a mile farther down" if Polihale became too crowded by a local. This is a terrific spot to relax, take in the sunset while sipping a drink or eating a picnic dinner, and watch the surf crash onto the sand. Except for shallow wading in the waves, it is not a nice area to be in the water. Watch the surf with one eye.

Investment is required to get there. To reach the beaches, you must first travel 5 miles on a very bumpy, pothole-filled road to the island's far west end along the south shore. UKG has clear instructions. There are numerous cautionary warnings, but if the road appears to be safe (i.e., dry enough), proceed cautiously and slowly. Driving to Polihale is frowned upon by rental car companies, but if you're feeling adventurous, it's a terrific trip.

Drive to the west coast of Kauai if you need some sun because it seems to be raining everywhere else. The driest parts of Kauai are located in the westernmost regions, including Polihale.

North Shore

Ke'e Beach

- Lounging
- Sunset (especially summer)
- Snorkeling
- Hiking

"Keh AY" when spoken. This is one of Kauai's most beautiful sunset locations, but getting there requires a drive, especially from the south shore. The physical end of the road is past Hanalei. Due to the presence of a protected reef, snorkeling is excellent here when the circumstances are favorable, especially during the summer. Here is also where the Kalalau Trail along the Na Pali coast begins.

Hideaways

1. Lounging
2. Seclusion
3. Swimming

Few people will go to Hideaways, a wonderful beach, if they aren't up for a difficult (though quick) climb. It is located in the Princeville area, and UKG offers detailed directions. Be cautious when entering the lake as the winters can be harsh.

Chapter 3:
Itineraries

Day 1: Arrival in Kauai

- Arrive in Kauai and check into your hotel or vacation rental.
- Relax on the beach and enjoy a traditional Hawaiian luau.

Day 2: North Shore Exploration

- Drive to the North Shore and visit Hanalei Bay.
- Hike the Kalalau Trail or explore the Na Pali Coast via a boat tour.
- Enjoy a seafood dinner at a local restaurant.

Day 3: Waimea Canyon

- Explore Waimea Canyon, often referred to as the "Grand Canyon of the Pacific."
- Hike some of the scenic trails in the area.
- Visit Waimea town for shopping and dining.

Day 4: East Side Adventures

- Head to the Wailua River and kayak to the Fern Grotto.
- Visit Opaekaa Falls and the nearby Hindu Monastery.
- Relax on Lydgate Beach Park.

Day 5: South Shore Relaxation

- Spend a day at Poipu Beach for sunbathing and snorkeling.
- Visit Spouting Horn Blowhole and Allerton Garden.
- Enjoy a beachfront dinner.

Day 6: West Side Adventure

- Take a helicopter tour to see the stunning landscapes of the Napali Coast.
- Explore the small town of Hanapepe and its art galleries.
- Sunset cruise along the coast.

Day 7: Departure

- Depending on your flight schedule, you may have some free time for shopping or beach relaxation.
- Depart from Kauai and head to the airport for your journey home.

Five days itinerary

Day 1: Lihue

- Morning: Arrive in Lihue and relax on Kalapaki Beach.
- Afternoon: Visit the Kilohana Plantation for a luau dinner.
- Evening: Check into your accommodation.

Day 2: North Shore

- Morning: Drive to the North Shore and hike the Na Pali Coast Trail (if experienced).
- Afternoon: Relax at Hanalei Bay and explore Hanalei town.
- Evening: Savor local Hawaiian dishes at a North Shore restaurant.

Day 3: Waimea Canyon

- Morning: Visit Waimea Canyon, often called the "Grand Canyon of the Pacific."
- Afternoon: Hike the Waimea Canyon Trail for stunning views.
- Evening: Return to your accommodation in Lihue or nearby.

Day 4: East Coast

- Morning: Explore Wailua Falls and kayak on the Wailua River to Secret Falls.
- Afternoon: Visit Opaekaa Falls and the Fern Grotto.
- Evening: Enjoy a sunset beach picnic.

Day 5: South Shore

- Morning: Relax on Poipu Beach and snorkel at Poipu Beach Park.
- Afternoon: Visit Spouting Horn and the Allerton Garden.
- Evening: Attend a traditional Hawaiian luau in Poipu.

Weekend itinerary

Day 1: North Shore

- Morning:
  - Start your day with a visit to Hanalei Bay and enjoy breakfast in Hanalei town.
  - Explore Hanalei Pier and Hanalei Valley Lookout.
- Lunch: Grab a plate lunch from a local food truck.
- Afternoon:
  - Hike the Kalalau Trail at Ke'e Beach or explore the Na Pali Coast by boat tour.
- Dinner: Dine at a seafood restaurant in Hanalei.

Day 2: Central Kauai

- Morning:
  - Drive to Waimea Canyon and take in the stunning views.
- Lunch: Picnic at Waimea Canyon State Park.
- Afternoon:
  - Visit Koke'e State Park and explore its hiking trails.
  - Stop at the Spouting Horn blowhole.
- Dinner: Head back to your accommodation or find a local restaurant.

Day 3: South Shore

- Morning:
  - Relax at Poipu Beach or visit Allerton Garden.
- Lunch: Enjoy lunch at a beachside cafe.
- Afternoon:
  - Snorkel at Lawa'i Beach or take a helicopter tour.
  - Explore Old Koloa Town.
- Evening: Watch the sunset at Shipwreck Beach.

Chapter 4:
Best Restaurants and Cuisine

A great gastronomic experience may be found on Kauai, where Hawaiian traditions are combined with a wide variety of foreign influences. For travelers to Kauai, here are some cuisines and culinary delights to try:

1. **Poke:** A traditional Hawaiian dish, poke (pronounced poh-kay), is a must-try when visiting Kauai. Fresh, raw fish that has been chopped up and marinated in a variety of tasty sauces is served over rice or as a salad. The fish is frequently ahi tuna or salmon. There are other varieties, such as spiciness, soy sauce-based shoyu, and limu (seaweed) poke.

2. **Plate Lunch:** A plate lunch is a quintessential Hawaiian comfort meal. It typically includes a protein (such as grilled or fried chicken, pork, or beef), two scoops of rice, and macaroni salad. Loco moco, a

popular variation, tops the rice with a hamburger patty, fried egg, and brown gravy.

3. **Kalua Pig:** Kalua pig is traditionally cooked in an underground oven called an imu. The result is tender, smoky, and delicious shredded pork. It's often served with cabbage and is a staple at Hawaiian luaus.

4. **Lau Lau:** Lau Lau is a Hawaiian dish consisting of pork, fish, or chicken wrapped in taro leaves and then steamed until tender. It's usually served with rice and has a unique, earthy flavor.

5. **Malasadas:** These Portuguese-inspired fried doughnuts are incredibly popular in Hawaii. They are light, fluffy, and coated in sugar. Some bakeries on Kauai offer malasadas filled with various flavors, like custard or lilikoi (passion fruit) cream.

6. **Shave Ice:** A refreshing treat, shave ice is finely shaved ice topped with a variety of flavored syrups. It's a perfect way to cool down on a hot day. Don't forget to ask for a scoop of ice cream or azuki beans at the bottom.

7. **Taro:** Taro is a staple in Hawaiian cuisine, and you'll find it in various forms, including poi (mashed taro root), taro chips, and taro pancakes. Poi is an acquired taste, so give it a try if you're feeling adventurous.

8. **Fresh Fruit:** Kauai offers an abundance of tropical fruits like pineapple, papaya, mango, lychee, and starfruit. Enjoy them fresh or in fruit salads and smoothies.

9. **Fish Tacos:** Kauai is known for its fresh seafood, and fish tacos are a popular way to enjoy it. Grilled or blackened fish, such as mahi-mahi or ono, is typically served in soft tortillas with fresh salsa and toppings.

10. **Hawaiian Luau:** Attending a traditional Hawaiian luau is a great way to experience an array of Hawaiian dishes, including kalua pig, poi, lomilomi salmon, and more. Luau events often include cultural performances and hula dancing.

11. **Kauai Coffee:** Kauai is home to some excellent coffee farms. Try the locally grown Kauai coffee, which is known for its rich and aromatic flavors. You can visit coffee plantations for tours and tastings.

12. **Farm-to-Table Cuisine:** Kauai has a growing farm-to-table food scene, with many restaurants sourcing ingredients locally. Be sure to explore the island's culinary diversity by trying dishes featuring fresh, local produce and seafood.

Kauai's cuisine offers a delightful fusion of flavors that reflect the island's unique culture and natural abundance. Whether you're savoring traditional Hawaiian dishes or exploring innovative creations, you're in for a culinary adventure on the Garden Isle.

Restaurants

Kauai offers a wide range of hotels, resorts, and accommodations to suit various budgets and preferences. Here are some notable hotels in Kauai, along with their renowned dishes or dining options:

1. **The St. Regis Princeville Resort:**
   - **Dining:** Makana Terrace is known for its breathtaking views of Hanalei Bay and its delicious seafood-focused menu. Try the Kauai shrimp or opah (moonfish) dishes.

- **Signature Drink:** The St. Regis is famous for its Sunset Ritual, where you can enjoy a champagne sabering ceremony while watching the sunset.

2. **Grand Hyatt Kauai Resort & Spa:**
   - **Dining:** Tidepools is a romantic, open-air restaurant set in thatched-roof huts overlooking koi-filled lagoons. The seafood and Pacific Rim cuisine, including macadamia nut-crusted mahi-mahi, is exceptional.
   - **Signature Drink:** Enjoy a Mai Tai or one of their tropical cocktails at the Stevenson's Library bar.

3. **Kauai Marriott Resort:**
   - **Dining:** Kukui's on Kalapaki Beach offers a variety of local dishes, including poke bowls, kalua pig tacos, and fresh seafood.
   - **Signature Dish:** Try their Ahi Poke Bowl, featuring marinated ahi tuna served with rice, seaweed salad, and tropical fruit.

4. **Sheraton Kauai Coconut Beach Resort:**
   - **Dining:** The Oasis restaurant serves Hawaiian-inspired dishes, including poke bowls, kalua pork sliders, and local fish dishes.
   - **Signature Dish:** The "Ahi on Fire" features seared ahi tuna with shichimi aioli and furikake rice.

5. **Koloa Landing Resort at Poipu, Autograph Collection:**
   - **Dining:** The Holoholo Grill offers a farm-to-table dining experience with a focus on fresh, local ingredients. Enjoy dishes like Kauai shrimp and taro-crusted ahi.
   - **Signature Dish:** Try the Koloa Landing Pupu Platter, a delicious assortment of local appetizers.

6. **The Westin Princeville Ocean Resort Villas:**

- **Dining:** Nanea Restaurant & Bar offers oceanfront dining and serves Hawaiian-inspired cuisine. Try their Kauai shrimp scampi or island fish.
- **Signature Drink:** Sip on a refreshing Lilikoi Margarita while taking in the view.

7. **Hanalei Bay Resort:**
   - **Dining:** While there is no on-site restaurant, you can dine at the nearby Princeville Resort or explore dining options in Hanalei town.
   - **Local Recommendation:** In Hanalei, don't miss the opportunity to try the famous Hanalei Taro & Juice Co. for taro-based dishes and refreshing juices.

8. **The Cliffs at Princeville:**
   - **Dining:** The Cliffs does not have an on-site restaurant, but you can enjoy meals in your condo or explore dining options in the Princeville area.
   - **Local Recommendation:** Try Piazza in Princeville for Italian cuisine or explore nearby restaurants like Hideaways Pizza Pub and Tiki Iniki for a variety of dishes.

Chapter 5:
Accommodations in Kauai

When visiting this picturesque island, finding the perfect accommodation is essential for an unforgettable experience. Here, we present ten of the best hotels in Kauai, each offering a unique blend of luxury, comfort, and breathtaking views.

1. **The St. Regis Princeville Resort** Located on the North Shore of Kauai, The St. Regis Princeville Resort offers unparalleled luxury. Perched on a cliff overlooking Hanalei Bay, this resort boasts elegantly appointed rooms, world-class dining, and a championship golf course designed by Robert Trent Jones Jr.

2. **Grand Hyatt Kauai Resort and Spa** Nestled on the sunny South Shore, the Grand Hyatt Kauai Resort and Spa is a tropical paradise. The sprawling property features lush gardens, a lazy river pool, and a saltwater lagoon. Guests can also enjoy the Anara Spa and numerous dining options.

3. **Koa Kea Hotel & Resort** This boutique oceanfront hotel in Poipu offers intimate and personalized experiences. With only 121 rooms, Koa Kea Hotel & Resort exudes tranquility and romance. Its Red Salt restaurant is celebrated for its farm-to-table cuisine.

4. **Kauai Beach Resort** Situated on 25 acres of lush beachfront property near Lihue, Kauai Beach Resort offers a blend of affordability and luxury. The property features multiple swimming pools, a spa, and easy access to the beach.

5. **Waimea Plantation Cottages** For a taste of old Hawaii, Waimea Plantation Cottages are a perfect choice. These historic cottages are set amid a 27-acre coconut grove on Kauai's sunny West Side. Guests can experience the charm of plantation life while enjoying modern amenities.

6. **The Cliffs at Princeville** Located on the North Shore, The Cliffs at Princeville offers spacious condo-style accommodations with stunning ocean views. The property includes tennis courts, a swimming pool, and a putting green.

7. **Kauai Marriott Resort** With a central location in Lihue, the Kauai Marriott Resort is a convenient base for exploring the island. It features a beautiful pool area, multiple dining options, and access to Kalapaki Beach.

8. **Aqua Kauai Beach Resort** This beachfront resort in Lihue offers a range of room options and amenities, including a spa, fitness center, and beachside bar. Aqua Kauai Beach Resort is an excellent choice for families.

9. **Hanalei Colony Resort** Located on the North Shore, Hanalei Colony Resort is a secluded getaway with a focus on natural beauty. The resort offers spacious

suites with kitchenettes and is near the charming town of Hanalei.

10. **Sheraton Kauai Coconut Beach Resort** Newly renovated and located on Kauai's eastern coast, the Sheraton Kauai Coconut Beach Resort offers modern comfort and beachfront access. It's an ideal choice for travelers looking to explore both the North and South Shores.

Chapter 6:
Cultural Activities in Kauai

Kauai, often referred to as the "Garden Isle" of Hawaii, is a paradise for nature enthusiasts and adventure seekers. While its natural beauty is undoubtedly its main draw, Kauai also offers a rich tapestry of cultural activities that allow visitors to connect with the island's history, traditions, and local way of life. In this comprehensive guide, we'll explore a wide range of cultural activities in Kauai that visitors should try, providing insights into the island's vibrant heritage.

1. Hula Dancing: Begin your cultural journey in Kauai by immersing yourself in the mesmerizing world of hula dancing. The ancient Hawaiian art form tells stories through graceful movements and gestures, and many resorts and cultural centers offer hula lessons and performances where you can learn the basics and watch professionals in action.

2. Lei Making: Lei making is a cherished Hawaiian tradition that involves creating intricate floral garlands. Participate in a lei-making workshop to learn the art of stringing beautiful flowers and leaves together, and take home your own handmade lei as a memento.

3. Hawaiian Language Lessons: Discover the essence of Hawaiian culture by learning the native language. Many cultural centers and educational institutions offer Hawaiian language classes, giving you the opportunity to connect more deeply with the island's heritage.

4. Luaus: Luaus are quintessential Hawaiian experiences. These festive gatherings feature delicious traditional Hawaiian cuisine, music, and hula performances. Attend a luau to savor dishes like kalua pig and poi while enjoying live entertainment.

5. Visit the Kauai Museum: For a comprehensive overview of the island's history and culture, spend some time at the Kauai Museum in Lihue. It showcases artifacts, artwork, and exhibits that provide insight into Kauai's past and present.

6. Polynesian Voyaging: Learn about the ancient art of Polynesian voyaging, which played a crucial role in Hawaiian history. Visit the Kauai Voyaging Society to explore traditional navigation techniques and the importance of the canoe in Hawaiian culture.

7. Cultural Workshops: Many cultural centers and organizations on the island offer workshops in traditional crafts like ukulele playing, lauhala weaving, and coconut husking. These hands-on experiences allow you to create your own souvenirs while gaining insight into local traditions.

8. Traditional Music: Listen to the soothing sounds of traditional Hawaiian music performed by local artists. Ukuleles, slack-key guitars, and sweet melodies create a relaxing and enchanting atmosphere.

9. Explore Historic Sites: Kauai is home to several historic sites that provide a glimpse into its past. Visit places like the Menehune Fishpond, ancient heiau (temples), and the Waioli Mission in Hanalei to learn about the island's early inhabitants and missionaries.

10. Local Farmers' Markets: Experience the flavors of Kauai by visiting local farmers' markets. Taste tropical fruits, sample freshly caught seafood, and engage with farmers and artisans to learn about their sustainable practices and cultural influences.

11. Kauai Art Tours: Discover the island's vibrant art scene by embarking on an art tour. Kauai boasts a community of talented artists whose works are inspired by the island's natural beauty and cultural heritage.

12. Cultural Festivals: Check the local events calendar for cultural festivals and celebrations. Festivals like the Kauai Coconut Festival and the Emalani Festival offer a deep dive into Hawaiian traditions, arts, and cuisine.

13. Traditional Canoe Rides: Take a traditional Hawaiian outrigger canoe ride to experience the ocean as ancient Hawaiians did. These guided tours often include stories about the island's seafaring history.

14. Storytelling Nights: Listen to captivating stories and legends of Kauai during storytelling nights. These gatherings provide insight into the island's folklore and the significance of storytelling in Hawaiian culture.

15. Cultural Shows: Attend cultural shows featuring hula, fire dancing, and other traditional performances. These events are not only entertaining but also educational, offering a glimpse into the island's history and legends.

16. Hawaiian Cuisine Cooking Classes: Learn to prepare authentic Hawaiian dishes during cooking classes offered by local chefs. Gain insights into the flavors and ingredients that define Hawaiian cuisine.

17. Volunteer Opportunities: Connect with the local community by participating in volunteer activities, such as beach cleanups, cultural preservation efforts, and conservation projects.

18. Traditional Healers and Medicine: Explore the practices of traditional Hawaiian healers, known as kahunas. Some practitioners offer workshops and sessions where you can learn about ancient healing techniques and the use of native plants for medicinal purposes.

19. Cultural Walks and Tours: Guided cultural walks and tours are available on the island. Knowledgeable guides share stories and historical facts about significant sites, providing context to your explorations.

20. Kauai's Unique Festivals: Don't miss Kauai's unique festivals, such as the Waimea Town Celebration, which commemorates Captain Cook's arrival in Hawaii, or the Eo e

Emalani i Alakai Festival, celebrating the last queen of Kauai. These events offer a taste of local traditions and history.

Chapter 7:
Nightlife And Festivals In Kauai

Kauai, the Garden Island of Hawaii, is renowned for its stunning natural beauty, lush landscapes, and pristine beaches. However, as the sun sets over this tropical paradise, the island comes alive with a vibrant nightlife scene that beckons visitors to experience a different side of Kauai. In this comprehensive guide, we will explore the various nightlife activities and joints that visitors must try while on the island, showcasing the diverse options for entertainment, dining, and socializing.

1. Beachfront Luaus:

Kauai offers an array of beachfront luaus that provide a unique blend of Hawaiian culture, delicious cuisine, and lively entertainment. One of the most popular luaus on the island is the Smith's Tropical Paradise Luau, where visitors can enjoy traditional hula dances, fire knife performances, and a sumptuous buffet feast. The Luau Kalamaku at Kilohana Plantation is another fantastic option, offering a theatrical luau experience with a historical twist.

2. Live Music and Dance:

For those seeking live music and dancing, Kauai offers an array of venues and events. Check out local bars and clubs like Rob's Good Times Grill in Lihue, which frequently hosts live bands and DJs, or Duke's Canoe Club in Lihue, where you can groove to the tunes of Hawaiian musicians while enjoying cocktails and ocean views.

3. Karaoke Nights:

Karaoke enthusiasts will find their groove in Kauai's nightlife scene. Many bars and lounges, such as Trees Lounge in Kapaa and Nawiliwili Tavern in Lihue, host karaoke nights where you can showcase your vocal talents or simply enjoy the lively atmosphere.

4. Sunset Cocktails:

The stunning sunsets in Kauai provide the perfect backdrop for sipping cocktails. Head to the St. Regis Princeville Resort's Makana Terrace for panoramic views of Hanalei Bay while savoring creative cocktails. Alternatively, RumFire Poipu Beach offers an extensive selection of craft cocktails and oceanfront seating to enjoy the sunset.

5. Dinner Cruises:

Experience romance and adventure with a dinner cruise along Kauai's picturesque coastline. Companies like Captain Andy's Sailing Adventures offer sunset dinner cruises that include gourmet meals and breathtaking views. You can also embark on a romantic evening sail with Holo Holo Charters for a memorable date night.

6. Tiki Bars and Exotic Drinks:

Embrace the tropical vibe at Kauai's tiki bars, known for their exotic cocktails and lively atmosphere. Tiki Iniki in Princeville serves up classic tiki drinks in a retro setting, while Lava Lava Beach Club in Kapaa offers beachfront dining and tropical libations.

7. Night Markets:

Kauai's night markets are a fantastic way to experience local culture and artisanal products. The Kauai Culinary Market in Poipu showcases the island's culinary talent with live cooking demonstrations, local food vendors, and music. Look out for other rotating night markets for handmade crafts, jewelry, and delicious street food.

8. Billiards and Sports Bars:

Sports enthusiasts can catch their favorite games and enjoy a game of billiards at Kauai's sports bars. JJ's Broiler in Lihue boasts a lively sports bar atmosphere with big-screen TVs, pool tables, and a menu of pub grub. It's a great place to unwind and root for your team.

9. Night Hikes and Stargazing:

Kauai's natural beauty extends into the night, making it an excellent destination for night hikes and stargazing. Guided tours like the Twilight Volcano Adventure by Hawaii Forest & Trail offer the opportunity to explore the island's unique nocturnal ecosystem and witness the starry skies from high altitudes.

10. Late-Night Food Trucks:

Craving a midnight snack? Kauai's food truck scene has you covered. Pono Market in Kapaa is famous for its delicious Hawaiian plate lunches served late into the night. Alternatively, visit the Sleeping Giant Grill in Wailua for mouthwatering tacos and burritos well past dinner time.

Kauai's nightlife scene offers something for everyone, whether you're looking for cultural experiences, live entertainment, or simply a relaxing evening by the beach. From beachfront luaus to tiki bars and night hikes, the Garden Island has an array of activities and joints that will make your nights in Kauai unforgettable. So, as the sun sets and the stars come out, don't miss the chance to explore the vibrant and diverse nightlife that this tropical paradise has to offer.

Festivals

Kauai, often referred to as the "Garden Isle," is not only known for its breathtaking natural beauty but also for its vibrant and culturally rich festivals. Nestled in the heart of the Hawaiian archipelago, Kauai offers a unique blend of tradition and modernity that comes alive during its numerous festivals throughout the year. Visitors to this tropical paradise have the opportunity to immerse themselves in a variety of festival activities that showcase the island's diverse culture, history, and natural wonders. In this comprehensive guide, we will explore some of the most captivating festival activities in Kauai that are a must-try for any traveler.

1. The Kauai Polynesian Festival

The Kauai Polynesian Festival is a celebration of the island's rich Polynesian heritage. Held annually, this festival transports visitors to a world of captivating dances, mesmerizing music, and mouthwatering Polynesian cuisine. The festival typically features performances from various Polynesian cultures, including Hawaii, Samoa, Tahiti, and New Zealand. Visitors can expect to witness the thrilling hula dances of Hawaii, the energetic Samoan fire knife dance, and the graceful Tahitian dance, among many others.

One of the highlights of the Kauai Polynesian Festival is the opportunity for visitors to participate in hula workshops, where they can learn the art of this traditional Hawaiian dance. Additionally, there are numerous food stalls offering Polynesian delicacies such as poi, laulau, and haupia for visitors to savor. The festival provides an immersive experience that allows travelers to gain a deeper understanding of the Polynesian culture that is an integral part of Kauai's identity.

2. Waimea Town Celebration

The Waimea Town Celebration is a beloved annual event that pays tribute to the history and culture of Waimea, a charming town on the western side of Kauai. This multi-day festival offers a wide range of activities and events that showcase the local community's spirit and heritage.

Visitors can enjoy a colorful parade featuring beautifully decorated floats, live music performances, and traditional Hawaiian games. The festival also includes a rodeo and paniolo (Hawaiian cowboy) competition, highlighting the island's ranching history. Food vendors serve up delicious Hawaiian plate lunches, while local artisans display their crafts at the festival's marketplace.

One of the standout attractions at the Waimea Town Celebration is the hoolaulea, a lively evening filled with music, dancing, and ono (delicious) food. Attendees can join in on the fun by learning to hula dance or trying their hand at playing traditional Hawaiian instruments. The sense of community and the warm aloha spirit make this festival a must-visit for anyone looking to experience the heart and soul of Kauai.

3. Eo E Emalani i Alakai Festival

The Eo E Emalani i Alakai Festival is a unique and enchanting celebration of Queen Emma, who visited the Alakai Swamp in 1871. This festival offers a glimpse into Kauai's history and celebrates the island's natural wonders. It takes place annually in October and is an unforgettable experience for those who appreciate both culture and nature.

Visitors to the festival can witness a reenactment of Queen Emma's journey to Alakai Swamp, complete with period costumes and traditional Hawaiian chants. The event also features guided hikes into the Alakai Swamp, allowing attendees to explore one of the world's most diverse and pristine ecosystems.

The Eo E Emalani i Alakai Festival is an opportunity to learn about the island's native flora and fauna, as well as its cultural history. Artisans and cultural practitioners demonstrate traditional crafts and activities, including lei-making and hula performances. This festival is a testament to the enduring connection between the people of Kauai and their natural surroundings.

4. Kauai Folk Festival

For lovers of folk music and Americana, the Kauai Folk Festival is a must-attend event. Held annually, this festival brings together talented musicians and enthusiasts from around the world for a weekend of live performances, workshops, and jam sessions.

Visitors to the Kauai Folk Festival can expect to hear a diverse range of musical styles, from bluegrass and folk to country and blues. The festival showcases both local talent and internationally acclaimed artists, creating a unique fusion of sounds and traditions.

In addition to the music, the festival offers workshops where attendees can learn to play various instruments, such as the ukulele and guitar. There are also dance workshops, storytelling sessions, and opportunities to engage with the artists through Q&A sessions. With its relaxed and friendly atmosphere, the Kauai Folk Festival is a delightful experience for music enthusiasts of all ages.

5. Koloa Plantation Days

Koloa Plantation Days is a week-long festival that commemorates the history of the sugar industry in Kauai and the diverse cultures that contributed to its success. This event takes place in the historic town of Koloa and offers a fascinating look into the island's plantation era.

One of the main highlights of Koloa Plantation Days is the historic walking tour, which guides visitors through the town's plantation-era buildings and landmarks. The tour provides insight into the lives of plantation workers and their contributions to Kauai's development.

The festival also features live entertainment, including traditional Hawaiian music and dance performances. Visitors can enjoy a taste of local cuisine at food booths offering dishes like saimin (noodle soup), malasadas (Portuguese doughnuts), and shave ice. Arts and crafts vendors showcase their work, and there are family-friendly activities such as games and contests.

Koloa Plantation Days is a wonderful opportunity to learn about Kauai's history while enjoying the festivities and flavors of the past.

6. Prince Kuhio Celebration

The Prince Kuhio Celebration is an annual event held in honor of Prince Jonah Kuhio Kalaniana'ole, a beloved figure in Hawaiian history who championed the rights of native Hawaiians. This celebration takes place in March and offers a unique opportunity to learn about the culture and heritage of the Hawaiian people.

Visitors to the Prince Kuhio Celebration can enjoy traditional Hawaiian music and dance performances, including hula and mele (song) competitions. There are also workshops on Hawaiian arts and crafts, where attendees can learn to make leis, lauhala (palm leaf) items, and other traditional crafts.

One of the festival's highlights is the ho'olaulea, a grand celebration featuring a luau with delicious Hawaiian food, cultural demonstrations, and a sense of community that reflects the spirit of aloha. This event not only pays tribute to Prince Kuhio but also serves as a reminder of the importance of preserving and perpetuating Hawaiian culture.

7. Annual Emalani Festival

The Annual Emalani Festival is a celebration of the historic journey of Queen Emalani, who traveled to Kokee in the 19th century. This festival, held in October, provides a captivating blend of history, culture, and nature.

Visitors can witness the reenactment of Queen Emalani's arrival in Kokee, complete with period costumes and traditional chants. The festival offers guided hikes through the stunning landscapes of Kokee State Park, allowing participants to appreciate the island's natural beauty and learn about its flora and fauna.

Cultural demonstrations and workshops are a significant part of the Annual Emalani Festival, where attendees can engage in traditional Hawaiian activities such as lei-making, lauhala weaving, and hula dancing. There are also live music performances, storytelling sessions, and educational talks that delve into Kauai's history and the legacy of Queen Emalani.

8. Kauai Chocolate & Coffee Festival

For those with a sweet tooth and a love for caffeine, the Kauai Chocolate & Coffee Festival is a delectable experience not to be missed. Held annually in Hanapepe, this festival celebrates the island's chocolate and coffee industries, showcasing the talent of local growers and artisans.

Visitors to the festival can enjoy tastings of a wide variety of chocolates and coffees, including unique flavors and blends that are exclusive to Kauai. Artisans and growers offer their products for sale, making it a great opportunity to bring home some island-inspired treats.

In addition to the culinary delights, the Kauai Chocolate & Coffee Festival features live entertainment, art exhibits, and workshops on topics like chocolate and coffee production. It's a delightful way to explore the island's flavors while supporting local businesses.

9. Kauai Steel Guitar Festival

The Kauai Steel Guitar Festival is a celebration of the distinctive Hawaiian steel guitar and its role in island music. This festival brings together steel guitar players and enthusiasts from around the world for a weekend of music and education.

Visitors to the Kauai Steel Guitar Festival can enjoy live performances by renowned steel guitarists, showcasing the instrument's unique and soulful sound. The festival often features workshops and masterclasses, allowing attendees to learn about the history and techniques of playing the steel guitar.

The laid-back and friendly atmosphere of the festival encourages jam sessions and collaboration among musicians and attendees. It's a great opportunity to immerse yourself in the world of Hawaiian music and experience the enchanting melodies of the steel guitar.

10. Annual Slack Key Guitar Festival

The Annual Slack Key Guitar Festival is a celebration of one of Hawaii's most iconic musical traditions: slack key guitar. Held in various locations on Kauai, this festival pays tribute to the art of playing the guitar with open tunings and fingerpicking styles.

Visitors to the festival can listen to performances by talented slack key guitarists, including both local legends and emerging artists. The festival often features workshops and demonstrations where attendees can learn about the history and techniques of slack key guitar.

One of the unique aspects of this festival is the sense of ohana (family) that permeates the event. Musicians and attendees come together to share their love for the music, creating a warm and welcoming atmosphere that embodies the spirit of aloha.

Conclusion

Kauai, with its stunning natural landscapes and rich cultural heritage, offers a wide array of festival activities for visitors to explore and enjoy. From traditional Hawaiian festivals that celebrate the island's history and culture to music festivals that showcase the talents of local and international artists,

Kauai's festivals provide a unique and immersive experience for travelers.

These festivals not only offer entertainment and cultural enrichment but also an opportunity to connect with the local community and gain a deeper appreciation for the traditions and natural beauty of the island. Whether you're interested in music, dance, history, or culinary delights, Kauai's festivals have something to offer everyone.

So, when planning your visit to the "Garden Isle," be sure to check the festival calendar and consider timing your trip to coincide with one of these vibrant and enriching events. It's a fantastic way to make your Kauai vacation an unforgettable experience filled with the spirit of aloha.

Chapter 8:
Souvenirs And Shopping in Kauai

Nestled in the heart of the Hawaiian archipelago, Kauai is a lush, tropical paradise known for its stunning landscapes, pristine beaches, and rich cultural heritage. However, beyond its natural beauty, Kauai also offers a delightful shopping experience that beckons visitors to discover unique treasures and souvenirs. In this guide, we will take you on a journey through the island's most enticing shopping areas, where you can immerse yourself in the island's culture and take home a piece of its beauty.

1. Historic Hanapepe Town

Our shopping journey begins in the charming Historic Hanapepe Town. Often referred to as "Kauai's Biggest Little Town," Hanapepe offers a delightful mix of art galleries, boutiques, and quaint shops. The town's historic charm is palpable as you stroll along the plantation-style storefronts and wooden boardwalks. Art enthusiasts will be captivated by the numerous galleries showcasing local talent, from traditional Hawaiian artists to modern creators. Don't forget to explore Friday Night Art Walk, a weekly event where you can meet local artists and enjoy live music.

2. Kauai Village Shopping Center

Heading eastward, we arrive at the Kauai Village Shopping Center, a modern shopping oasis in Lihue. Here, you'll find an array of upscale boutiques, restaurants, and specialty shops. From high-end fashion to Hawaiian-inspired jewelry, Kauai Village offers a diverse shopping experience. After indulging in some retail therapy, unwind at one of the waterfront restaurants and savor fresh seafood while gazing at the scenic Nawiliwili Bay.

3. Kapaa Town

Continuing along the eastern coast, we reach Kapaa Town, a vibrant hub of activity. Kapaa is renowned for its unique blend of boutique shops, thrift stores, and local markets. Coconut Marketplace, a must-visit, boasts an array of artisans and crafters selling handmade goods, perfect for picking up authentic Kauai souvenirs. Additionally, the town hosts a weekly farmer's market, where you can taste fresh island produce and mingle with the locals.

4. Poipu Shopping Village

Venturing to the southern coast, Poipu Shopping Village beckons with its open-air shopping experience. Amidst the lush gardens and koi ponds, you'll find boutique clothing stores, art galleries, and gift shops. The village also hosts weekly hula shows and live music, adding to the festive atmosphere. After shopping, take a short walk to Poipu Beach

Park to relax on the golden sands or watch the sunset over the Pacific Ocean.

5. Princeville Center

Heading north, Princeville Center awaits, nestled amidst the stunning backdrop of the North Shore's lush green mountains. This shopping destination offers a range of boutiques, surf shops, and restaurants. Peruse the upscale boutiques for island-inspired fashion and jewelry, or grab a smoothie and soak in the panoramic views of Hanalei Bay. With its picturesque location, Princeville Center combines shopping with scenic beauty.

6. Hanalei Town

Continuing along the North Shore, we arrive at the picturesque Hanalei Town. This historic village is surrounded by the dramatic mountains of the Na Pali Coast and offers a unique shopping experience. Stroll along the main street lined with boutiques, art galleries, and specialty shops. Hanalei is known for its handcrafted goods, so be sure to explore the local artisans' creations, from jewelry to pottery. While in town, savor a Hawaiian shave ice and take in the laid-back, tropical atmosphere.

7. Waimea Town

Our shopping journey takes us to the west coast, where Waimea Town awaits. This historic town offers a glimpse into Kauai's past with its plantation-style architecture. Antique shops and thrift stores are scattered throughout the town, inviting you to discover vintage Hawaiian memorabilia and unique finds. While here, don't miss the chance to visit the

Waimea Canyon, often called the "Grand Canyon of the Pacific," to witness awe-inspiring natural beauty.

8. Art Walks and Local Markets

Beyond these specific shopping areas, Kauai also hosts various art walks and local markets that are worth exploring. Keep an eye out for events like the Kauai Art Tour, where you can visit local artists' studios and purchase their creations directly. The Kilauea Art Night is another delightful event, offering an opportunity to discover local art and enjoy delicious food from food trucks.

In conclusion, Kauai's shopping areas provide a diverse and captivating experience for visitors. From the historic charm of Hanapepe to the coastal elegance of Poipu, and the artistic flair of Kapaa, the island offers something for every shopper. Whether you're in search of unique souvenirs, high-end fashion, or handmade crafts, Kauai's shopping areas beckon you to explore, indulge, and take home a piece of this enchanting island's spirit. So, as you plan your visit to Kauai, make sure to set aside some time to immerse yourself in its shopping delights and discover the treasures that await you on this tropical paradise.

Souvenirs

One of the best ways to remember your Kauai experience is by bringing home souvenirs that encapsulate the spirit of the island. In this comprehensive guide, we'll explore 20 must-have souvenirs from Kauai and where to find them.

1. Kauai Coffee:

Kauai is renowned for its coffee, and a bag of locally grown beans is the perfect way to start your souvenir collection. Kauai Coffee Company, located in the town of Kalaheo, offers a wide variety of coffee flavors, including their famous Kauai Blue Mountain coffee. You can also visit their visitor center for tours and tastings.

2. Hawaiian Quilts:

Hawaiian quilts are a unique and beautiful souvenir to bring home from Kauai. These quilts often feature intricate, nature-inspired designs. You can find them in various stores and boutiques across the island, including the Kauai Quilt Museum in Lihue.

3. Aloha Shirts:

Aloha shirts, also known as Hawaiian shirts, are a classic souvenir choice. These colorful, floral-printed shirts are perfect for capturing the island's laid-back vibe. You can find them in many shops, but Coconut Style in Kapaa is a popular spot for high-quality aloha shirts.

4. Koa Wood Products:

Koa wood is native to Hawaii and is used to create beautiful, handcrafted items such as bowls, jewelry, and furniture. Look for Koa wood products at shops like Martin & MacArthur, located in various locations around the island.

5. Macadamia Nuts:

Hawaii is famous for its macadamia nuts, and Kauai is no exception. You can find an assortment of macadamia nut products, including flavored nuts, chocolates, and cookies, at grocery stores, farmers' markets, and specialty shops.

6. Ukuleles:

The ukulele is a symbol of Hawaiian music and culture. Purchase a ukulele as a souvenir and even take lessons to learn to play it during your stay. Try The Ukulele Store in Kapaa for a wide selection.

7. Tiki Decor:

Tiki decor items, such as tiki mugs, statues, and torches, are a fun and kitschy way to remember your time in Kauai. You'll find a variety of tiki-themed souvenirs at Tiki Mania in Kapaa.

8. Hawaiian Jewelry:

Hawaiian jewelry often incorporates traditional symbols and materials like seashells, pearls, and black coral. Explore local jewelry stores like Hanalei Strings in Hanalei or Banana Wind in Kapaa for unique pieces.

9. Lei:

Leis are a symbol of Hawaiian hospitality and are commonly given to visitors as a warm welcome. You can find leis at various flower stands and shops throughout the island, especially at Lihue Airport.

10. Sea Glass Jewelry:

Kauai's coastline is a treasure trove of sea glass, which local artisans use to create stunning jewelry. Look for these unique pieces at shops like Kauai Sea Glass in Hanapepe.

11. Hawaiian Art:

Hawaiian art, including paintings, prints, and sculptures, reflects the island's natural beauty and culture. Galleries like the Kauai Society of Artists in Lihue showcase the work of local artists.

12. Hula Implements:

Hula is an integral part of Hawaiian culture, and you can find hula implements like grass skirts, leis, and drums at many souvenir shops and markets across the island.

13. Handmade Soap:

Treat yourself to locally made soap infused with tropical scents like plumeria, coconut, and pineapple. Shops like Island Soap & Candle Works in Kilauea offer a wide range of options.

14. Kauai Salt:

Kauai is home to salt ponds that produce high-quality sea salt. Purchase some Hawaiian salt as a culinary souvenir and add a touch of Kauai to your cooking. Look for it at local markets and specialty food stores.

15. Shells and Shell Jewelry:

Kauai's beaches are a haven for seashell collectors. You can find beautiful seashell jewelry or even collect your own shells to create a unique keepsake.

16. Aloha Spirit Wear:

Aloha spirit wear includes items like hats, visors, and beach bags with the word "Aloha" emblazoned on them. These make for excellent gifts and can be found in many stores across the island.

17. Pineapple Products:

While Kauai isn't as famous as other Hawaiian islands for pineapples, you can still find pineapple-themed products like jams, sauces, and even pineapple-shaped ceramics in various gift shops.

18. Surf Memorabilia:

Kauai is known for its excellent surf spots. Bring home a piece of the island's surf culture with surf-themed souvenirs, such as surfboard keychains, t-shirts, or vintage surf posters.

19. Coconut Products:

Coconut-based products are popular in Kauai. You can find coconut oil, lotions, and even coconut-based snacks like coconut chips and macaroons in local stores.

20. Hand-Painted Coconuts:

For a truly unique souvenir, consider purchasing a hand-painted coconut. Local artists often paint vibrant scenes and designs on coconuts, making them a one-of-a-kind keepsake.

Where to Find These Souvenirs:

Now that you know what souvenirs to look for, let's explore where to find them on the island:

1. **Local Markets:** Kauai has numerous local markets and farmers' markets where you can find a variety of souvenirs, including fresh produce, handmade crafts, and jewelry. Some popular markets include the Kauai Community Market in Lihue and the Hanapepe Art Night.
2. **Souvenir Shops:** Throughout Kauai, you'll find souvenir shops that cater to tourists. These shops often carry a wide range of souvenirs, from t-shirts and postcards to unique handcrafted items.
3. **Art Galleries:** Kauai boasts a thriving art scene, and you can discover a wealth of Hawaiian art and crafts in galleries across the island. Check out the galleries in Hanapepe, Hanalei, and Kapaa for beautiful pieces created by local artists.
4. **Specialty Stores:** For specific souvenirs like Koa wood products, Hawaiian quilts, and sea glass jewelry, you may need to visit specialty stores or boutiques that focus on these items. Many of these stores are located in towns like Hanalei, Kapaa, and Koloa.
5. **Cultural Centers:** Consider visiting cultural centers and museums like the Kauai Museum in Lihue or the

Kauai Cultural Center in Hanapepe. These places often have gift shops where you can find unique cultural souvenirs.

6. **Beachside Stands:** Some of the best souvenirs in Kauai can be found at beachside stands or pop-up shops near popular beaches. Keep an eye out for these as you explore the island.

Chapter 9:
Tips For Traveling in Kauai

Here are tips for travelers in Kauai to save money, ensure safety, and make the most of their trip:

Ten Money-Saving Tips:

1. **Travel During the Off-Peak Season:** Accommodations and activities are often cheaper during the shoulder or off-peak seasons, typically in spring and fall. Avoid the busiest times, such as major holidays, to get better deals.
2. **Book in Advance:** Plan and book your accommodations, flights, and activities well in advance to secure lower prices and avoid last-minute surcharges.
3. **Cook Your Own Meals:** Consider staying in accommodations with kitchen facilities and prepare some of your meals. Local farmers' markets offer fresh produce and affordable options for groceries.
4. **Use Coupons and Discounts:** Look for coupons, deals, and discount cards for restaurants, tours, and activities. Check local tourist information centers for current offers.
5. **Rent a Car Off-Airport:** Renting a car away from the airport can sometimes save you on airport surcharges and rental fees. Plus, it gives you the flexibility to explore the island at your own pace.
6. **Take Advantage of Free Activities:** Enjoy Kauai's natural beauty by hiking, swimming, or exploring beaches, waterfalls, and trails, which are often free or have minimal entry fees.

7. **BYOB (Bring Your Own Beach Gear):** Purchase or bring your own snorkel gear, beach chairs, and umbrellas instead of renting them at beachside vendors.
8. **Shop Local:** Support local businesses and artisans by shopping at farmers' markets and craft fairs for souvenirs and gifts. You may find unique items at lower prices.
9. **Pack Light:** Avoid baggage fees by packing light and efficiently. Many Hawaiian outfits are casual, so you won't need an extensive wardrobe.
10. **Use Public Transportation:** If you're staying in a central location, consider using public buses or shuttles for short trips instead of renting a car for the entire stay.

Ten Time-Saving Tips:

1. **Plan Your Itinerary:** Create a daily schedule and prioritize activities to make the most of your time on the island.
2. **Book Tours and Activities Online:** Reserve tours, excursions, and activities in advance through reputable websites to save time and secure your spots.
3. **Arrive Early:** Visit popular attractions early in the morning to avoid crowds and maximize your experience.
4. **Use GPS and Maps:** Download maps and navigation apps on your smartphone to help you navigate the island's roads and trails efficiently.
5. **Pack Light and Smart:** Pack only what you need to streamline airport security checks and make it easier to move around.
6. **Consider Guided Tours:** Join guided tours for certain activities, such as hiking or snorkeling, to save time on planning and logistics.

7. **Travel During Off-Peak Hours:** When driving, avoid peak traffic hours, especially in and around larger towns like Lihue and Kapaa.
8. **Opt for Direct Flights:** Whenever possible, choose direct flights to Kauai to minimize layover and travel time.
9. **Prep for Airport Security:** Arrive at the airport with plenty of time to spare and prepare for security checks by having your ID and boarding passes ready.
10. **Stay in a Central Location:** Choosing accommodations in a central area like Kapaa can save commuting time when exploring different parts of the island.

Five General Tips to Know:

1. **Respect the 'Aloha Spirit':** Embrace the spirit of 'Aloha' by being respectful, kind, and considerate to locals and fellow travelers.
2. **Pack Sun Protection:** Protect yourself from the strong Hawaiian sun with sunscreen, sunglasses, and wide-brimmed hats. Stay hydrated throughout the day.
3. **Observe Wildlife Ethically:** When encountering wildlife, maintain a safe distance and do not disturb or feed animals, including Hawaiian monk seals and sea turtles.
4. **Practice 'Leave No Trace':** Follow eco-friendly practices by disposing of trash properly and leaving natural areas as you found them.
5. **Learn Basic Hawaiian Phrases:** While English is widely spoken, learning a few Hawaiian phrases like "Aloha" (hello/goodbye) and "Mahalo" (thank you) can enhance your experience and show respect for the local culture.

Conclusion

In summary, a trip to Kauai is a trip to a tropical paradise with unparalleled natural beauty, cultural diversity, and aloha attitude. Travelers will have a one-of-a-kind and enduring experience in Kauai because to its beautiful scenery and energetic local culture. Be sure to sample the island's delectable cuisine, interact with the friendly residents, and gather sentimental mementos that encapsulate the spirit of this Hawaiian treasure while visiting this wonderful island. Everyone can find something to enjoy on Kauai, regardless of their interests — adventure seekers, nature lovers, or those just looking to unwind. So pack your luggage, take in the Garden Isle's natural beauty, and make lifelong memories. Aloha!

Made in the USA
Las Vegas, NV
10 January 2024

84169957R00056